WARTIME SPIES

CREATIVE EDUCATION • CREATIVE PAPERBACKS

WORLD
WAR I SPIES

MICHAEL E. GOODMAN

Published by Creative Education and Creative Paperbacks
P.O. Box 227, Mankato, Minnesota 56002
Creative Education and Creative Paperbacks are imprints of
The Creative Company
www.thecreativecompany.us

Design and production by Chelsey Luther
Art direction by Rita Marshall
Printed in Malaysia

Photographs by Alamy (akg-images, PRISMA ARCHIVO), Central
Intelligence Agency (CIA Library/Freedom of Information Act
Reading Room), Corbis (adoc-photos, Bettmann, Heritage Images,
Hulton-Deutsch Collection, SUSANNAH IRELAND/epa, Sean
Sexton Collection, Swim Ink 2 LLC, Underwood & Underwood, US
ARMY/SCIENCE PHOTO LIBRARY, Zimmer/dpa), Getty Images
(Mondadori, Popperfoto, Print Collector), Library of Congress (Penn
State University Libraries), Lost & Taken (Brant Wilson), Newscom
(Mirrorpix), TextureX.com (TextureX), VectorTemplates.com

Library of Congress Cataloging-in-Publication Data
Goodman, Michael E.
World War I spies / Michael E. Goodman.
p. cm. — (Wartime spies)
Summary: A historical account of espionage during World War I,
including famous spies such as Mata Hari, covert missions, and tech-
nologies that influenced the course of the conflict.
Includes bibliographical references and index.
ISBN 978-1-60818-602-0 (hardcover)
ISBN 978-1-62832-207-1 (pbk)
1. World War, 1914-1918—Secret service—Juvenile literature. 2.
Spies—History—20th century—Juvenile literature. I. Title. II. Title:
World War One spies.

D639.S7G67 2014
940.4'85—dc23   2014037535

CCSS: RI.5.1, 2, 3, 5, 6, 8; RH.6-8.3, 4, 5, 6, 7, 8, 9

First Edition HC 9 8 7 6 5 4 3 2 1
First Edition PBK 9 8 7 6 5 4 3 2 1

CONTENTS

A SPY UNCOVERED

The man's passport identified him as an American named Charles Inglis. But he was really Carl Hans Lody, a German-born spy. For several months, Lody had been observing British warship movements in English ports and sending coded telegrams to his *handler* in Germany. Lody, who had been given very little spy training, didn't realize his messages were being intercepted and read by British *counterespionage* agents. Most of the messages contained harmless or wrong information, and British *agents* let them go through to Germany. In September 1914, Lody, worried about being discovered, decided to flee to Ireland. He sent off one last detailed report to Germany. This one contained valuable military information. The message was stopped, and British agents soon tracked Lody down in Ireland and brought him to London to stand trial. He was imprisoned in the Tower of London. On November 6, 1914, Lody faced a firing squad, becoming the first spy executed by the British in World War I.

COMPLEX ALLIANCES LEAD *to* WAR

IN THE EARLY 1900S, European powers competed with each other for land, power, and resources. Great Britain, France, and Germany wanted to control areas in Africa and the Middle East. Austria-Hungary and Russia were vying for domination in the Balkan countries of southern Europe. Adding to the rivalry between nations were strong feelings of distrust. Many countries established alliances with each other, promising to step forward if one of them was attacked by an enemy. Europe was a powder keg just waiting to explode.

The fuse on that keg was lit on June 28, 1914, when Serbian *nationalist* Gavrilo Princip assassinated Archduke Franz Ferdinand,

Meant to allow friendly greetings with passersby, the archduke's open car proved deadly instead.

the heir to the Austro-Hungarian throne, in Sarajevo, Bosnia. Austria-Hungary blamed Serbia for the act and declared war on Serbia exactly one month later. That started a chain reaction: Serbia had an alliance with Russia, so the Russians declared war on Austria-Hungary. Because France had an alliance with Russia, it joined the war on Serbia's side, too. Meanwhile, Germany came out in support of Austria-Hungary, its partner in another alliance, and declared war on Russia and France. When German troops moved into *neutral* Belgium on the way toward France, Great Britain honored its own agreement to protect Belgium by declaring war on Germany. By September 1914, most of Europe was at war. The main combatants were the Central Powers (Germany, Austria-Hungary, and Turkey) and the Allied Powers (Britain, France, Russia, and—later—Italy). Soon, blood would be shed in many parts of the world.

One country that decided to stay on the sidelines—at least for the time being—was the United States. A great deal of political pressure would be put on U.S. president Woodrow Wilson to join the Allied Powers. Another type of pressure would be exerted by German espionage agents in the U.S. trying to undermine any American efforts to help the Allies. Both sides wondered what America would do.

COVERT OPS
SUCCESS ON THE SECOND TRY

The assassination of Archduke Franz Ferdinand didn't go as planned on June 28, 1914. Members of the Serbian terrorist group the Black Hand were assigned to attack the archduke as he traveled through Sarajevo that day. The first man lost his nerve and let the royal party drive right by him. The second threw a bomb at the wrong car and seriously wounded two of Franz Ferdinand's close friends. Later, the archduke insisted on visiting his wounded friends at the hospital. It was during that second trip that Gavrilo Princip spotted the archduke's car and fatally shot the Austrian heir and his wife.

CHAPTER ONE

PROFESSIONAL SPIES *on the* JOB

The RMS Olympic, *a "sister" ship of the ill-fated* Titanic, *served as a troopship during the war.*

ALONG WITH FORMING ALLIANCES in the years before World War I, European nations also began an arms race. Munitions factories churned out guns and ammunition; shipyards manufactured warships; even some early airplanes were equipped for wartime use. The arms race was public knowledge. Behind the scenes, another kind of buildup was going on. Military leaders began posting spies undercover in their rivals' territory. They hoped to discover secrets that would give them an edge if their countries went to war.

Although spies had been employed in wartime for thousands of years, peaceful espionage was a new development. So were full-time professional spies. In the past, most wartime spies were either soldiers persuaded to go undercover in enemy territory or civilian (non-military) volunteers. Some *operatives* were paid, but most did not make their living by spying or by catching spies. Now, the field of espionage was changing.

In 1909, Great Britain established its first official *intelligence* organization, called the Secret Service Bureau. It consisted of two

WWI guns were classified according to the sizes of their shells, such as the six-inch guns in the foreground.

departments—the Foreign Section to handle intelligence gathering and covert (undercover) operations and the Home Section to deal with catching spies and stopping attacks within the country.

One of the main reasons Britain created the Secret Service Bureau was because its military leaders suspected that professional spies from other countries, namely Germany, were already working inside Great Britain. They were right. Members of a German *spy ring* were prowling around British ports and navy yards or engaging workers in conversations. They were trying to find out all they could about Britain's ships and then sending reports back to their bosses in Germany. At the time, Britain had the world's most powerful navy, but Germany was not far behind in military capability.

Some spy ring members had been living in England for many years and had unusual *covers*. For example, Karl Gustav Ernst worked as a hairdresser in London. He also played the special spy role of "postman." Ernst would receive packages from Germany containing letters to distribute to other members of the ring. He would put the letters into new envelopes, stick on British stamps, and place them in the ordinary London mail. That way, nosy postal workers wouldn't become suspicious that certain people were receiving a lot of mail from Germany. Ernst relayed spy reports

back to Germany in the same way.

Ernst tried to be careful, but Home Section agents were already tracking his activities. They began surveilling him after a leading German military officer had been spotted at his barbershop. Soon, the Home Section (which had only 17 members at the time) was tracking several dozen suspected German agents. Early in the morning of August 4, 1914, the same day Great Britain declared war on Germany, British police across the country raided several locations and arrested Ernst and 20 other members of the spy ring. Government lawyers presented enough evidence to convict 13 of the suspected agents as spies. Germany never set up another ring in Britain during the war, but a few individual operatives continued

More than 2 million British men volunteered to serve in the military, perhaps thanks to social pressure.

COVERT OPS
A SPY IN THREE WARS

Few spies stayed on the job as long as South African Frederick "Fritz" Duquesne. In 1899, he spied and fought against the British in the Boer War. He resurfaced again as a German *saboteur* in World War I. He claimed to have planted a bomb in 1916 that sank a ship carrying the British War Secretary, Lord Kitchener. More than 25 years later, Duquesne turned up in the U.S. as the leader of a German spy ring at the start of World War II. This time, he was captured and imprisoned for most of the rest of his life.

BOERS IN BATTLE
BURGHERS SLAAGS.

VAN HOEPEN

In the Boer War of 1899–1902, members of the citizen army of South Africa were called "burghers."

to spy on British shipping nonetheless. One of those operatives was Carl Hans Lody.

Not all spies or counterintelligence experts in World War I were either German or British. In northern France, a woman named Louise de Bettignies set up a ring of agents to spy on the German forces occupying her country. She used the code name Alice Dubois, and her ring was known as the "Alice Service." A French woman named Marthe Betenfeld Richer acted as a *double agent*, spying for France and pretending to spy for Germany. She hindered German war efforts by stealing samples of the invisible ink their spies used and by passing along disinformation—fake intelligence—that fooled her German employers. An Argentine woman named Maria de Victorica traveled to Ireland to spy for Germany. Her plan was to undermine the British by helping Irish rebels fight for their independence from Great Britain. In Palestine (now Israel), a group of Jewish settlers formed a spying network called "Nili" to report on the activities of Turkish troops who were controlling their country. Their reports helped the British eventually drive out the Turks.

The Russians had an important double agent based in Austria-Hungary before the war began. He was Alfred Redl, the head of Austria-Hungary's military intelligence. The Russians blackmailed Redl into turning over secret documents, including his nation's plans to invade Serbia, should war break out in the Balkans. When Austria-Hungary did attack Serbia in the first weeks of the war, the Russians were prepared and easily defeated them.

Most double agents spoke several languages fluently and were skilled at blending into their surroundings, even in a foreign country. Most were also given training in *tradecraft* before they were sent into the field. Tradecraft included learning how to develop a cover, how to spot and avoid a *tail*, how to write messages in code and *decipher* them, and how to set up and use *dead drops* to convey and receive messages.

Some agents were well trained, but others were not. Two agents who became famous for their mistakes were an exotic dancer from Holland known as Mata Hari and a German *diplomat* named Wilhelm Wassmuss.

Mata Hari's real name was Margaretha Zelle. She first made headlines performing sexy dances throughout Europe. Mata Hari believed she could use her beauty and charm to be an effective spy. At first, she agreed

Mata Hari lived in Indonesia in the 1890s, where she learned some of the traditional dances.

to spy for the Germans against the French. Then she was caught by the French authorities and quickly agreed to change sides and spy for them against the Germans. The French sent her on an assignment to meet a German officer in Spain and trick him into revealing secrets about German strategy. The officer saw through her ruse and decided to trap her instead. He sent a message to Germany that he knew the French would intercept, asking for money to pay Mata Hari for her spy work for Germany. When the dancer crossed the border, the French arrested her as a double agent and sentenced her to death by firing squad. Many historians believe that Mata Hari was executed not because she was really a double agent but because French leaders wanted to show their citizens that they had captured and killed a "notorious" spy.

Wassmuss was not as famous as Mata Hari, but the mistake he made had a much greater impact on the war. He worked for the German embassy in Persia (now Iran), but his real mission was to organize Arab leaders to fight against the British in the Middle East. One of his undercover assignments involved printing *propaganda* leaflets that claimed that the British were against Islam, the major religion of the Middle East. The Germans hoped Arabs would read the pamphlets and declare a holy war against Britain. That never happened. Instead, the British marched successfully through Persia and closed in on the town where Wassmuss was hiding. He packed quickly and fled, but in his haste, he left behind his copy of a codebook used by German diplomats for secret messages. The book helped codebreakers in England decipher many German communications during the rest of the war, including the infamous Zimmermann Telegram, which you will read about later.

Before the British captured it in 1917, Baghdad, Iraq, was the southern capital of the Ottoman Empire.

17

CHAPTER TWO
INKS, PIGEONS, *and* OTHER SPY TOOLS

THERE WAS A WIDE range of spies operating around the world during the "Great War," and they were using some unusual tools— or variations on old standbys—to help them in their work. One good example was invisible ink. Spies have been using invisible ink solutions for hundreds of years. In fact, a Latin historian named Pliny the Elder, writing in the first century A.D., described using ink made from the "milk" of a certain plant. The messages seemed to disappear as the ink dried but could be made visible by gently heating the paper on which the message was written. Other types of invisible ink were made from certain chemical solutions. A reader had to brush the letter with a second chemical mixture to make the hidden words reappear.

During World War I, spies took the concept of writing messages in invisible ink to a new level. Some succeeded in keeping their messages secret, while others did not. One of those who failed was a German man named Carl Muller. He arrived in London in 1915 and took up what seemed to be an ordinary correspondence with "friends" in Germany. In between the lines of his normal-sounding letters, he included information about British troop and ship movements. The spy information was written in an ink made from lemon juice that

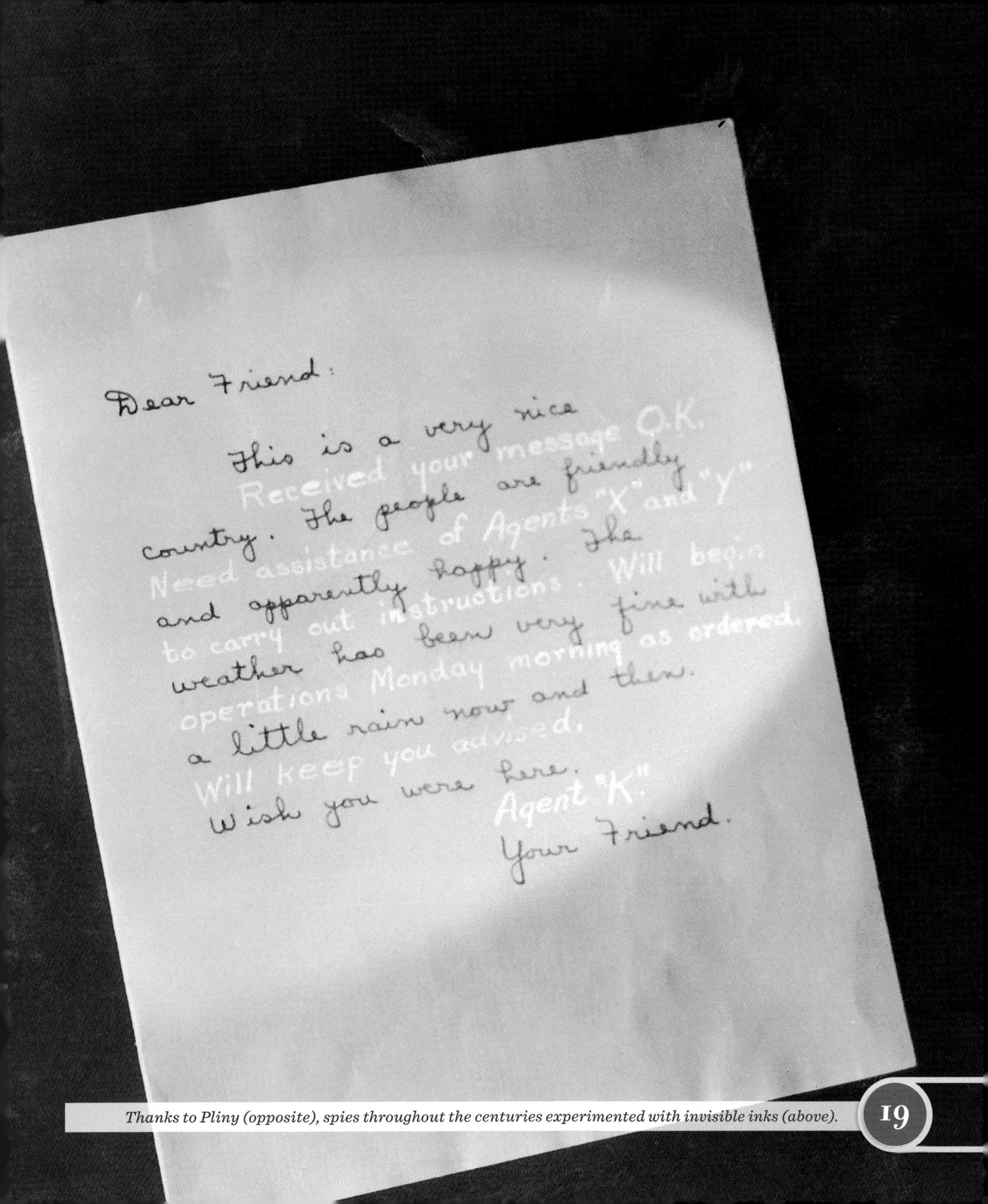

Dear Friend:

    This is a very nice country. The people are friendly and apparently happy. The weather has been very fine with a little rain now and then. Wish you were here.

    Received your message O.K. Need assistance of Agents "X" and "Y" to carry out instructions. Will begin operations Monday morning as ordered. Will keep you advised.

               Agent "K"

               Your Friend.

Thanks to Pliny (opposite), spies throughout the centuries experimented with invisible inks (above).

disappeared after it dried. Some of Muller's letters were intercepted by a group of postal censors, who tested the paper for invisible ink. In one letter, they discovered a hidden message noting that "15,000 troops left yesterday for France from Southampton" (a large English port city). The Secret Service Bureau began

tracking Muller's every move, and a few weeks later, they arrested him

A ready supply of ammunition was vital to soldiers on the front lines—but it was conspicuous.

at his apartment. When they inspected the premises, they discovered a supply of lemons, an address book, and several pens whose tips were black from being exposed to an acid such as lemon juice. Muller even had a lemon in his coat pocket. When questioned, Muller said he used lemon

juice to keep his teeth clean, an obvious lie. Muller was arrested, tried, and sentenced to death by firing squad.

A music hall performer in England named Courtney de Rysbach was both an unlikely spy and an unlikely person to be caught writing secret messages in invisible ink. Rysbach was an English citizen whose parents were Austrians. When the war broke out, he was touring in Germany. German officials stopped him as he attempted to leave the country and threatened to send him to a prison camp. They offered to free him if he agreed to become a spy in England. Rysbach received training in creating an ink from toothpaste mixed with a chemical called potassium ferrocyanide. When the ink was brushed with an acidic liquid called ferric chloride, it would turn blue and be readable. Rysbach used the ink to write messages between the lines of music from his act. One time, he tried to mail several sheets of music paper to an address in Germany, but his package was stopped and inspected. The inspectors discovered a secret message in which Rysbach offered to send valuable information about British navy movements if he were sent more money. Soon, Rysbach was under arrest and headed to a British prison.

One of the most unusual invisible ink stories of World War I involved Maria de Victorica. In addition to her espionage work in Ireland discussed earlier, Victorica also spied for Germany in the

CHEMICALS AND CONSPIRACIES

Mabel Elliot had always liked chemistry. In 1915, she put her chemistry knowledge to use and helped expose several undercover German spies in England. Elliot, who spoke fluent German and Dutch, was working as a censor, reading letters addressed to foreign locations in an effort to spot suspicious communications. She was troubled about one letter mailed to Holland and decided to apply heat to the paper. Suddenly, additional words appeared that provided details about soldiers protecting London. She turned the letter over to British intelligence, and a suspected German spy was arrested. Elliot later exposed two more spies in the same way.

With so many British men marching off to war, women joined police forces and took various jobs.

U.S. during the war. She used a special ink that she soaked into silk scarves. She would then allow the scarf to dry, press it with a cool iron, and then wear it around her neck. When she had a message to write, she would dip the scarf in water, wring it out, and use the liquid as her ink. Unfortunately for Victorica, members of a special Secret Ink Bureau in the U.S. War Department found a way to expose her invisible ink. When they did, they discovered a disturbing message about bombings being planned in the U.S. and several other countries. Victorica, too, was headed for prison.

Victorica's scarves were unusual, but some spies found even more inventive ways to get their messages to their contacts. A few wrote information on their bodies, which led government agents to stop some suspected spies in train stations or at border crossings and make them take off their clothes and undergo a thorough inspection. One spy was even found to have written messages in tiny print on his toenails. A chemical applied to his nails brought out the writing.

Using the mail or personal messengers were normal ways to convey secret information. A more unusual method involved using carrier pigeons. Messages would be placed in tiny capsules attached to a pigeon's leg. Then the pigeon would fly to a place where it had been trained to go. As many as 500,000 pigeons were used for spying missions during the war. They would sometimes be transported to enemy-occupied areas by plane and dropped in using tiny padded parachutes. Field agents would collect the pigeons and care for them until the birds were needed to carry messages back home.

Once the U.S. entered the war in 1917, American army divisions also employed pigeons on the battlefield. One bird even earned a medal for bravery. The pigeon was named Cher Ami, which means "dear friend" in French. He delivered 12 important messages between American forces fighting near Verdun, France. On his last mission, Cher Ami was shot in the breast and leg but still got through. The message he delivered came from a commander whose division was trapped by the enemy. A few hours later, many of the soldiers from the division had been rescued. Cher Ami recovered from his wounds and received a medal for his heroic service.

*The French army trans-
ported their messenger
pigeons using trucks
such as this one.*

An 1880s English model of a pocket watch camera served as a forerunner to more modern versions.

Telephones were routinely used by all sides in the war to transmit messages from army headquarters to the front lines. But enemy fire often destroyed telephone wires, and commanders worried that phone lines could be tapped. So some army units would write messages, roll them up, and place them in the base of a missile that would be fired to its intended readers. A flare attached to the missile would go off to signal its arrival at the destination.

There were some other ingenious methods used by World War I spies to convey secret communications. Coded messages were sometimes printed in tiny letters on the backs of buttons sewn onto coats or jackets. Pocket watches with small hidden compartments were also used by some agents. The Germans even invented a tiny camera concealed in a pocket watch. The winding stem was really a lens, and a small button at the base could be pressed to take a picture.

A pair of Dutch operatives working for Germany thought they had the perfect way to transport secrets. They opened a cigar business in the harbor city of Portsmouth, England, and imported Dutch cigars there. They didn't hide the messages inside cigars. Instead, they used their orders for cigars as codes for communicating how many warships and merchant ships they observed moving in and out of the harbor. Unfortunately for the spies, their code was broken, and they soon faced a firing squad.

An extreme form of military and wartime punishment, execution by firing squad is called fusillading.

25

CHAPTER THREE

FEMALE SPIES— FRONT *and* CENTER

IN WARS BEFORE THE 1900s, women generally played a minor role, even in the area of espionage. In World War I, however, women spies moved front and center. A good example was Louise de Bettignies. She was brought up in a wealthy family in the town of Lille in northern France and then attended Oxford University in England, where she studied languages. She spent several years as a teacher and governess (private tutor) before returning to Lille. When the war broke out, she volunteered as a Red Cross nurse but longed for more excitement. German troops occupied Lille, and de Bettignies made note of everything they did. Then she decided to take her information to the British Secret Service Bureau in London. She boarded a ferry bound for England and simply walked into the bureau's office. British espionage leaders were impressed with her spy work and put her through a tradecraft training program. She returned to France and established a cover as a lacemaker named Alice Dubois.

Dubois then built her own spy network, which the British and French referred to as the "Alice Service." It included a chemist who mixed special inks for messages and forged identification cards; a mapmaker who made detailed charts and could write a 1,600-word

As Germany occupied more European cities (opposite), pleas for Americans to help increased.

message in the space of a postage stamp; and a special assistant who kept everything organized. Eventually, the Alice Service had 20 members. They helped rescue and smuggle out Allied soldiers imprisoned by the Germans. They also communicated with each other and their handlers through messages hidden in balls of wool, small toys, chocolate bars, and even artificial limbs.

German intelligence officers knew a spy ring was active in Lille, but it took them more than a year to locate and capture de Bettignies/ Dubois. She was thrown into the St. Gilles military prison in Belgium, where she was forced to live in terrible conditions for more than two years. She became sick and died just days before the end of the war. In 1927, a statue was erected in Lille to honor her memory.

French-born Marthe Betenfeld Richer was another exceptional Allied operative in World War I. Like de Bettignies, she came from a wealthy family. A daring and adventurous person, Richer was one of the first women in France to fly an airplane. After her husband, who was also a pilot, was killed early in the war, Richer was recruited by French intelligence. She agreed to move to Spain, where she posed as a bored, rich woman. She met many German diplomats and military leaders in Spain and began dating a German naval captain. When he asked her to return to France as a spy for Germany, Richer was thrilled at the idea of becoming a double agent. Over the next few months, she was able to pass along valuable "inside information" to the French. Once, she even brought them samples of German invisible ink via tablets hidden underneath her fingernails. French chemists figured out the ink's formula and were able to read messages they intercepted that were written using that ink. Richer also agreed to pass along messages that French intelligence agents invented to misdirect the Germans.

Richer served as a double agent for the rest of the war, operating from France, Brazil, and Argentina. Did Richer ever do real spy work for the Germans? No one knows for sure. She claimed after the war that she had remained loyal to France. The Germans paid her a lot of money, she said, but she turned it all over to her French handlers. In the 1930s, French leaders honored Richer for her intelligence work by naming her to the French Legion of Honor. When war broke out

nor
uel Church

retary to Gov-
lecture at the
Church last
at it is brought
one generation
ers of the coun-

trip of the Lib-
continent, and
descriptions of
d in a number
te, showing by
ayed by some of
me to view the
ecture last night
iven in this city
e trip and was
ices of the Im-
Church men's

ROBBED

April 7.—Money
the value of more
e reported miss-
-Barre post office
nd a systematic
has failed to bring
The checks and
sent to department
or mail orders, but
score or more that
as been presented

EATHER

and vicinity: In-
udiness to-night,
wed by rain Satur-
change in tempera-
-night about freez-

nsylvania: Increas-
to-night; Saturday
fresh north to east

river and all its
continue to fall
next twenty-four
rain indicated for
probably be suffici-
a general rise in all
e system by Satur-
Sunday. A stage of
eet is indicated for
Saturday morning.

al Conditions
tern storm has mov-
iddle Gulf region. It
light to moderately
in the Middle West
The front of the
ressure area from the
has advanced to the
antic coast, causing a
1 of 2 to 20 degrees in
e east of the Ohio
the Lake Region, with
emperature in Central
ru New York, in West-
ylvania and through-
enter part of the Lake

e: 8 a. m., 36.
5:33 a. m.; sets, 6:36

Detectives Would Have Complete Census Made of Harrisburg's Slums

Following an inspection of "slums"
in parts of the Eighth and Ninth
Wards and in North Seventh street by
members of the city detective bureau,
a request will be made to Mayor Meals
to permit the detectives taking a cen-
sus of the city's "slums."

During the inspection four detectives
say they saw conditions that are worse
than the East Side of New York. In
many places sewage was dumped into
the street, it is said, and at another
place black and white people were found
under the same roof. In North Seventh
street a foreign family was found who
used their bath tub as a garbage col-
lecting device.

At many places users of dope were
found, and these places will be sub-
jected to further investigation, it is
said.

SUSPECT YOUTH MURDERED

Marks On Body Throw Doubt On Sui-
cide Pact Theory

Pottsville, Pa., April 7.—While State
police were dragging the Schuylkill
river yesterday for the body of 14-
year-old Helen Hepler, supposed to
have died in a suicide pact with Clay-
ton Mengel, evidence developed that
Mengel had a rival who was forcing
his attentions upon Miss Hepler.

The body of Mengel, which was
dragged from the river, was found to
have marks of violence upon it. Sur-
geons say these wounds could not have
been inflicted while the body was in
the river, and the police say Mengel
may have been murdered and his body
thrown into the river.

COUNTRY HOMES ROBBED
By Associated Press

Highland Falls, N.Y., April 7.—It
was discovered early to-day that the
country homes of Herbert L. Satterlee,
son-in-law of the late J. P. Morgan,
and Mrs. Jennie Bigelow Tracy, daugh-
ter of the late John Bigelow, had been
forcibly entered by thieves. Both families being away, the amount of valu-
ables believed to have been stolen will
not be definitely known until their
return.

BILL TO PROMOTE DODD
By Associated Press

April 7.—A bill

With the co-operation of city
ministers, school board officials, sup-
erintendents of the two Y. M. C. A.'s
and the Y. W. C. A. and the managers
of motion picture theaters assured,
Dr. J. M. J. Raunick, city health officer, to-day made an appeal to parents to keep their children from going
into other people's homes until the
measles epidemic has been checked.
Dr. Raunick said to-day that despite

[Continued on Page 13]

THREE WOMEN ARE IN GERMAN TOILS; ONE IS EXECUTED

Belgian Killed For Treason, Two Others Given Terms in Prison, Is Assertion

By Associated Press

Amsterdam, Holland, April 7, via
London.—The assertion is made by
the Echo Belge that Miss Gabrielle
Petit, of Molenbeek, Belgium, has been
put to death by Germans after trial by
court-martial on a charge of treason.
It is alleged she conducted an information bureau in the interest of
German's enemies.

The newspaper also states that
Louise de Bettignies, of Lille, has been
sentenced to death, but that the sentence has been commuted to imprisonment for life.

Another woman, Marie Van Houtte,
the newspaper says, has been sentenced to imprisonment for fifteen
years.

Cost Him Fifty Dollars to Use a "Turkey Call"

Important arrests in Perry county
were made by Charles B. Baum, State
game protector, for violations of the
game laws. John D. Titzel, of near
New Germantown, Perry county,
charged with using a turkey call October 15, yesterday was fined $50. H.
C. Showaker, of the same place, was
fined $25 for shipping a wild turkey
out of the State.

PRETTIEST BRIDE OF YEAR
GETS LICENSE TO-DAY: ONLY 15

The prettiest bride-to-be of the year
(the clerks in the marriage bureau
said she was the prettiest, anyway)
got a license to-day to wed a man
just twice her age. The girl is Carolyn
of this city, who called at the

---

day was responsible for the
nation of the Governor not to
withdraw from the fight. These newspaper stories intimated that he was
being forced to surrender to the Republican organization and this in-
terpretation of his probable action in
the hope of restoring harmony has
aroused all the combativeness of his
nature. It is also reported that he

(Continued on Page 17.)

C. Ross Boas Buys Old Gutelius Store; to Build August 1

C. Ross Boas, one of the city's
leading jewelers, who for more than
twenty years has conducted his place
of business at 214-216 Market street,
has purchased the "Gutelius Store"
property at 28 North Second street,
and about August 1 he will begin work
on the erection of a modern apartment and store building.

"The first floor store will be occupied by our own store, of course,"
said Mr. Boas.

The Gutelius notion store property
is a little 90-year-old frame struc-
ture owned by Henry M. and Mary
Oliver. They are residents of Clark's
Valley, back of Dauphin. The con-
sideration was not made public. The
property got its name from the fact
that for many years it has been occupied by the Misses Jennie and Ellen
L. Gutelius. Their little place of business was one of the most exclusive of
its kind in the city and even since the
death of Miss Jennie Gutelius a few
years ago, the surviving sister has
maintained a store that is still patron-
ized by the older families.

The Harrisburg Trust Company
owns the present store room of Mr.
Boas but he plans to move as soon
as his new quarters are ready. The
Gutelius lease doesn't expire until
August 1. The deal was closed, according to Mr. Boas to-day through
John W. Reily. The property has a
frontage of 25 feet and a depth of 97
feet.

Senator Harding of Ohio Chosen Temporary Chairman of Republican Convention

Chicago, Ill., April 7.—Senator War-
ren G. Harding, of Ohio, was selected
temporary chairman of the Republican national convention by unani-
mous vote of the subcommittee on ar-
rangements of the Republican national
committee to-day on the first ballot.

Other convention officers were
chosen as follows: Lafayette B. Glea-
son, of New York, secretary; William
F. Stone, of Baltimore, sergeant-at-
arms, and George L. Hart, of Roanoke,
Va., official reporter.

FEELS HONORED
By Associated Press

Washington, D. C., April 7.—Senator
Harding, notified of his selection, accepted and received congratulations

---

of Verdun the Germans have
the line of their attack slightly to the
east, driving against the lines between
Bethincourt and Chattancourt and
penetrating a first line trench there.

The locality is in the vicinity of
Dead Man's hill, where Germans and
French have been battling at intervals

[Continued on Page 6.]

PORCH-WINDOW BOX PLAN GETS BOWMAN'S O. [

President of Chamber of Commerce Sends Strong Letter Will Decorate Store

Chamber of Commerce endo
ment for the Telegraph's porch
window box contest was forthco
to-day in the form of a letter fron
president, J. William Bowman.

Mr. Bowman speaks vigorously
the beautification of the city by
ers during the summer months,
just to show that he means pre
what he says he let it be known

[Continued on Page 6.]

Body of Unidentified, Well-Dressed Man Fou by Crew in Paxton C

Lying partly immersed in the
creek near the bridge along the
delphia and Reading Railway
near Berryhill street, the body
unknown man was found this n
by a train crew just about to le
yards.

The man was well dressed,
a black cheviot suit with patch
a new pair of black shoes, size
shirt with narrow black str
black bow necktie. A pair
noseglasses and an old knife
only articles found in the poc
small gold ring was found on
finger of the right hand, but
ting had been lost.

Coroner Eckinger was ca
turned the corpse over to C
Mauk, undertaker, Sixth an
streets, where it may be view
morgue. The authorities ar
every effort to have the c
identified. He is 5 feet in
about 110 pounds, is about
old, has a brown mustache
hair tinged with gray. It
lieved that the body was in
more than three days, and
of violence were found duri
amination. The city and
thorities are not positive w

---

*When Louise de Bet-
tignies was sentenced to
prison, another female
spy was executed.*

again in 1939, the renowned 50-year-old spy came out of retirement to work in the French *Resistance*.

Elsbeth Schragmüller, one of the best-known German *spymasters* in World War I, grew up in a middle-class family in the town of Schlüsselburg in central Germany. She was a brilliant student and was especially good at learning languages. After finishing grade school, she became one of the first women in her region accepted into an advanced college program. She eventually became a college professor.

When the war began, Schragmüller joined the army as an office worker and asked to serve at the front in Belgium. There, she met a German commander in the hallway of a headquarters building and urged him to let her become a spy. Her initiative impressed the commander, and he sent her to a tradecraft training program. She did so well during her training that her bosses decided to make her a teacher instead of an agent. She was sent to Antwerp, Belgium, to set up her own spy school. She was a demanding teacher, and her students became known for their professionalism.

Schragmüller ran the school until nearly the end of the war. She then retired and became a professor again in Germany. She also wrote articles and books about spying and spy training. In one article, she explained why women might be better suited than men for intelligence

work: According to Schragmüller, spy work required empathy [emotional understanding],

Germany made use of recently developed airships called zeppelins to bomb cities during the war.

good organizational skills, the ability to adapt to changing conditions during a mission, and an intuition about how to coax others to perform and do their best. In all these areas, she concluded that women were often more highly skilled or better suited than men.

No undercover agent in World War I came to a more tragic or emotional end than Edith Cavell. Born in England, Cavell was serving as a teacher and nurse in Brussels, Belgium, when the war began. After German troops occupied Brussels, Cavell helped form an underground

In 1917, the U.S. War Department set up a special division to study codes and secret inks being used by other countries' spies. Staff members in the Secret Ink Bureau of MI-8 were given detailed instructions on how to reveal messages written in invisible ink. Suggestions included dusting the paper surface with powdered charcoal, running a hot iron over the surface without scorching the paper, or using one of several different chemicals that might break down substances used to conceal the writing. There were even instructions on how to open and reseal a letter without being detected.

--5--		100 cc.
Water		3 gm
Potassium bromide		3 gm
Copper sulphate		
--6--		100 cc.
Water		2.5 gm
Nickel chloride		2.5 gm
Nickel nitrate		
--7--		3 gm
Nickel chloride		3 gm
Cobalt chloride		100 cc.
Water		

Samples 1, 4, and 5 will doubtless exert a very corrosive action on steel pens, and therefore if suitable in other respects would have to be used with a quill pen.

If I observe any other samples which seem to possess any particular advantage, I will let you know, or if you will tell me just what characteristics you desire such a product to have, I will try to reproduce it,

Respectfully,

A M Heinzelmann

Asst. Chemist.

CONFIDENTIAL

The last of the WWI documents to be declassified were those describing secret writing methods.

organization to smuggle trapped Allied soldiers into neutral Holland. The group helped more than 700 soldiers escape. Cavell was warned several times to leave Belgium, but she stayed to continue her work.

In August 1915, a German patrol raided one of the "safe houses" where soldiers were hidden until they could be helped out of the country. They discovered papers that identified Cavell and other members of the underground organization. She was immediately arrested and admitted her part in helping soldiers escape. She was found guilty of treason (according to the military law of the occupying German force) and executed 10 weeks later.

After the sentence was carried out, the Germans decided to use Cavell's execution as a lesson to others who might want to help Germany's enemies. They distributed propaganda posters throughout German-occupied territories to stress the warning. Their plan backfired, though. The Allies responded with posters of their own, honoring Cavell and condemning her death as murder. In the U.S., the *New York Times* ran a front-page story on her execution and follow-up reports on the reaction to it. In England, Cavell was viewed as a hero, and many young men were encouraged to enlist in the army to fight the "evil" Germans who had killed her.

Cavell's death quickly became a symbol of how terrible war could be for those who wanted only to do what was right. American poet Robert Underwood Johnson wrote that she was "Black War's white angel ... whose pure heart harbored neither hate nor blame." Monuments honoring Cavell were built in Belgium, Great Britain, and France. One of the peaks in the Canadian Rocky Mountains was renamed Mount Edith Cavell, and several streets in Europe, Canada, and South Africa were named in her honor.

A devoted nurse, Cavell was later reported to have said, "I can't stop while there are lives to be saved."

CHAPTER FOUR

SPIES *from the* MIDDLE EAST *to* AMERICA

ARMIES FROM MANY DIFFERENT nations took part in World War I, and there was spying going on in many different parts of the world. A lot of the espionage activity took place in the U.S., with the Allied Powers trying to push the U.S. to enter the war, and the Central Powers working to keep U.S. troops at home. Ireland and the Middle East were also hotbeds of espionage.

The Middle East was a particularly strategic area that both sides in the war hoped to control. It not only had valuable oil resources, but it also was a vital key to shipping in the region, thanks to the Suez Canal. It was a place that attracted archaeologists and religious pilgrims, too. The Ottoman (Turkish) Empire had ruled countries in the Middle East for many years, but the British and Germans were hoping to take charge there now.

Britain sent in a number of archaeologists who doubled as spies when they weren't digging for ancient artifacts. One of the most colorful of these figures was T. E. (Thomas Edward) Lawrence. Lawrence, who spoke fluent Arabic, helped organize an Arab revolt against the Turks in the Sinai Desert (between present-day Egypt and Israel). His raiding parties wrecked bridges and blew up trains,

The city of Port Said, Egypt, was established as the Suez Canal underwent construction (1859–69).

T. E. Lawrence first traveled to the Middle East as a college student in 1909 and became fascinated.

cutting supply lines that the Turks used. On one mission in Palestine, Lawrence was captured. He was wearing Arab robes, but his bright blue eyes gave away his European background. He was tortured but didn't reveal any information. Luckily, he managed to escape and return to England. He became known around the world as "Lawrence of Arabia." An exciting movie of the same name and based on his exploits won an Academy Award for Best Picture in 1962.

German spies were also very active in Ireland. Irish ports were critical for shipping across the Atlantic, and Irish nationalists were a big annoyance to the British. German spies did what they could to help these Irish rebels in their fight for independence from Great Britain. They hoped the rebels would distract British forces that might otherwise be used to fight in Belgium and France. When the rebels did stage the short-lived Easter Rising in 1916 (April 24–29), many of the weapons they used were smuggled into Dublin with the help of German spy Maria de Victorica.

There is not much evidence of Irish spies who were active during World War I, but one Irishman in England played a major role in the British Secret Service Bureau. William Melville from County Kerry in southwestern Ireland began his career as a policeman with Scotland Yard. Then he turned his focus to counterespionage. He was one of the first members of the Secret Service Bureau when it was formed in 1909. Melville headed up a special spy-hunting section of the Bureau and was the person who identified hairdresser Karl Gustav Ernst as the "mailman" for a German spy ring operating in England. After the war, he founded a spy school to train counterespionage agents.

During the Easter Rising, Irish rebels occupied Dublin's post office, which was shelled by the British.

While German spies were active in both England and Ireland, they were especially busy in America. The U.S. took an officially neutral stance in the war at first, but American industries contributed food, weapons, and other supplies to the Allied Powers. Germany was interested

COVERT OPS
CHOCTAW COMMUNICATORS

Battling in France in October 1917, American soldiers needed to ensure their telephone communications would not be decrypted. One American officer realized that he had several American Indians from the Choctaw tribe in his regiment. There were Choctaws serving in other regiments as well. They spoke a unique language that the Germans would not be able to understand. Nineteen of the Choctaw soldiers stepped forward as "code talkers," and they were used to relay strategic messages to each other over the phone. The Germans were completely confused, and the Choctaw communications played a vital role in several Allied victories.

American Indians were not required to join the military, but many served with distinction.

in cutting off these supply lines. Spies were planted inside the U.S. to carry out sabotage missions, and German submarines, called U-boats, were sent out into the North Atlantic Ocean. The U-boats had permission to blow up any vessel—even passenger ships—that came through the area.

One of the first U-boat targets was the *Lusitania*, which set out from New York on May 1, 1915, for Liverpool, England. In the weeks before the *Lusitania* sailed, the German government placed notices in newspapers, warning passengers that vessels might be attacked. The ship's owners decided that their luxury liner would have enough protection from the British navy to get through safely, and nearly 2,000 passengers boarded. On May 7, a U-boat discharged a torpedo at the *Lusitania* approximately 11 miles (17.7 km) south of Ireland. The boat sank quickly, and more than 1,200 passengers drowned, including 128 Americans. The sinking of the *Lusitania* outraged many Americans, but the country was still not ready to join the war.

Meanwhile, pro-German saboteurs were at work inside the U.S. A German businessman named Franz von Rintelen moved to America in 1915 to set up an export company. He hoped to use funds supplied by Germany to buy up food and guns that might be sent to the Allies across the Atlantic. Then Rintelen decided that it would be easier just to blow up the supplies. He developed special time-delayed explosives, called pencil bombs, and used them to destroy as many as 35 ships in American harbors. Rintelen also traveled to Ireland to set off bombs there, but he was followed by British counterespionage agents and eventually sent to jail.

Pencil bombs played a key role in another act of sabotage that took place in New Jersey near the Statue of Liberty. In the early hours of July 30, 1916, two German agents named Lothar Witzke and Kurt Jahnke set off several bombs that started fires inside a large ammunitions depot on Black Tom Island. More than 2 million pounds (907,185

Although there were 48 lifeboats, only 6 were launched before Lusitania sank within 18 minutes.

kg) of explosives were stored in warehouses on Black Tom, and when the fires ignited them, the blast was so powerful that it shattered windows in office buildings in New York City and the vibrations could be felt more than 100 miles (161 km) away in Maryland.

The *Lusitania* and Black Tom incidents nearly drove the U.S. into the war, but resistance to getting involved was still strong. Then came the Zimmermann Telegram, a coded communication sent in January 1917 by German foreign minister Arthur Zimmermann to the German embassy in Mexico City. It was picked up unexpectedly by British **cryptanalysts** in London, who were able to decode the message, thanks in part to the codebook left in Persia by Wilhelm Wassmuss. (Remember that incident from earlier in this book?)

The telegram explained that Germany intended to engage in new U-boat attacks and worried that the U.S. might decide to go to war against Germany as a result. So Zimmermann wanted his diplomats to meet with Mexican leaders and ask them to invade the U.S. from the south, should America decide to enter the war. Zimmermann believed the invasion would force the U.S. to keep its troops at home. In return, Zimmermann promised that Germany would financially support the invasion and help Mexico regain the territory that it had previously lost to the U.S., including the states of New Mexico, Texas, and Arizona.

The analysts turned the decoded telegram over to British government leaders, who decided to send a copy to President Wilson in Washington, D.C. An angry Wilson soon called on Congress to declare war on Germany, which it did on April 6, 1917. Once U.S. troops entered the war, the Allies began a steady drive toward victory. Amazingly, the careful work of a small group of codebreakers in London was instrumental in bringing America into the war and helping to end one of the world's most destructive conflicts.

Jersey City firefighters worked to put out the blazes following the explosion on Black Tom.

THE WORLD *at* PEACE?

AT 11:00 A.M. ON the 11th day of the 11th month in 1918, fighting in World War I came to an end. The war officially concluded with the signing of the Treaty of Versailles seven months later.

It had been a terrible conflict in which nations discovered new ways to kill and wound through the use of poison gas attacks, tanks, and airplanes. In all, more than 65 million soldiers, sailors, spies, and other combatants took part in the conflict. More than 8.5 million

Britain and France built tanks to provide a means of mobile protection to soldiers fighting in trenches.

people were killed, more than 21 million were wounded, and an additional 7 million went missing or were held as prisoners of war. And those figures don't even account for the 10 million-some civilians who were killed or injured.

After the war, empires crumbled and boundaries were redrawn. The empires of Russia, Austria-Hungary, and Germany were dismantled or lost lands to the creation of new countries, and the Ottomans lost their grip in the Middle East as Turkey gained independence by 1923. President Wilson proposed his "Fourteen Points" program for world peace, which included the formation of a so-called League of Nations. The organization never really took hold despite the world's high hopes for peace.

World War I was called the "War to End All Wars," but that is not what happened. Instead, some of the anger and ambition that had led up to war in 1914 was left to simmer in the defeated nations such as Germany and Austria. A new power—Japan—was building in the Far East, and a new political regime had taken over in Russia. All these forces would come together to ignite yet another world war just 20 years later.

COVERT OPS
DILLY'S ALL WET

Alfred Dillwyn "Dilly" Knox was one of the most successful and most peculiar British cryptanalysts of all time. Before the war, Dilly studied Latin and Greek. When the war broke out, he used his language skills on codebreaking. Dilly did his best thinking while soaking in a bathtub. He sometimes would soak and think for hours at a time. A special bathtub was set up in the naval command building in London for Dilly to sit in as he studied coded enemy messages. It must have worked. Dilly is credited with cracking several "unbreakable" enemy code systems in both world wars.

WORLD WAR I
TIMELINE

JUNE 28, 1914 — Austrian Archduke Franz Ferdinand and his wife Sophie are assassinated by a Serbian nationalist in Sarajevo, Bosnia.

JULY 28, 1914 — Austria-Hungary declares war on Serbia.

AUGUST 1–3, 1914 — Germany declares war on Russia and France.

AUGUST 4, 1914 — Germany invades Belgium, and Great Britain declares war on Germany. British agents and police arrest 21 suspected German spies in England.

AUGUST 6, 1914 — Austria-Hungary declares war on Russia, and Serbia declares war on Germany.

AUGUST 19, 1914 — U.S. president Woodrow Wilson announces American neutrality.

SEPTEMBER 5, 1914 — The First Battle of the Marne begins, marking the start of trench warfare.

FEBRUARY 4, 1915 — Germany begins a submarine blockade of Great Britain, even firing on neutral vessels.

APRIL 22, 1915 — The Second Battle of Ypres begins. The Germans first use poison gas.

MAY 7, 1915 — The British ocean liner *Lusitania* is sunk by the German U-boat *U-20*.

OCTOBER 12, 1915	British nurse and resistance leader Edith Cavell is executed by a German firing squad.
JULY 30, 1916	Explosives at a warehouse on Black Tom Island in New Jersey are detonated by German spies.
SEPTEMBER 15, 1916	During the Battle of the Somme, tanks are used for the first time in any war.
JANUARY 19, 1917	Germany sends the secret Zimmermann Telegram to Mexico. It is intercepted and deciphered by the British.
MARCH 15, 1917	Russian Tsar Nicholas II abdicates, or gives up the throne.
APRIL 6, 1917	The U.S. declares war on Germany.
NOVEMBER 7, 1917	Bolshevik revolutionaries successfully overthrow the Russian government.
NOVEMBER 9, 1918	German Kaiser Wilhelm II abdicates and flees Germany.
NOVEMBER 11, 1918	Germany signs an agreement to end the fighting.
JUNE 28, 1919	The Treaty of Versailles is signed, and World War I officially ends.

GLOSSARY

AGENTS—people who work for an intelligence service; spies

COUNTERESPIONAGE—efforts made to prevent or block spying by an enemy

COVERS—made-up occupations or purposes of agents

CRYPTANALYSTS—experts at translating secret messages into normal language

DEAD DROPS—secure locations that usually include a sealed container where spies and their handlers can exchange information or intelligence materials to avoid meeting in person

DECIPHER—to convert a coded message, or cipher, into normal text

DIPLOMAT—someone who represents a nation's government while serving in another country

DOUBLE AGENT—a spy who pretends to work for one country or organization while acting on behalf of another

HANDLER—a person who trains or is responsible for spies working in a certain place

INTELLIGENCE—information of political or military value uncovered and transmitted by a spy

NATIONALIST—someone who supports his or her country winning its independence from another country

NEUTRAL—not taking sides in a conflict or argument

OPERATIVES—secret agents working for an intelligence group

PROPAGANDA—material distributed to promote a government's or group's point of view or to damage an opposing point of view; some propaganda is untrue or unfairly exaggerated

RESISTANCE—an organized underground movement or people fighting against a foreign power occupying their country

SABOTEUR—someone who intentionally destroys railroads, ships, bridges, or machinery for a political purpose

SPY RING—a group of spies working together to carry out espionage

SPYMASTERS—people who recruit and are in charge of a group of spies

TAIL—someone who is following a spy working undercover

TRADECRAFT—the procedures, techniques, and devices used by spies to do their work

SELECTED BIBLIOGRAPHY

Crowdy, Terry. *The Enemy Within: A History of Espionage*. Oxford: Osprey, 2006.

Hastedt, Glenn. *Espionage: A Reference Handbook*. Santa Barbara, Calif.: ABC-CLIO, 2003.

Hunter, Ryan Ann. *In Disguise! Undercover with Real Women Spies*. Hillsboro, Ore.: Beyond Words, 2013.

Janeczko, Paul B. *The Dark Game: True Spy Stories*. Somerville, Mass.: Candlewick Press, 2010.

Macrakis, Kristie. *Prisoners, Lovers, and Spies: The Story of Invisible Ink from Herodotus to al-Qaeda*. New Haven, Conn.: Yale University Press, 2014.

Price, Bill. *Spies of the First World War*. London: RW Press, 2013.

Proctor, Tammy M. *Female Intelligence: Women and Espionage in the First World War*. New York: New York University Press, 2003.

Sulick, Michael J. *Spying in America: Espionage from the Revolutionary War to the Dawn of the Cold War*. Washington, D.C.: Georgetown University Press, 2012.

WEBSITES

BRITISH NATIONAL ARCHIVES: FIRST WORLD WAR
http://www.nationalarchives.gov.uk/pathways/firstworldwar/
Online exhibitions that cover a wide range of topics related to British history, including spying in World War I.

NATIONAL WOMEN'S HISTORY MUSEUM SPIES EXHIBITION
http://www.nwhm.org/online-exhibits/spies/2.htm
Brief biographies of notable women spies and descriptions of their espionage activities from the American Revolution to the Cold War.

NOTE: Every effort has been made to ensure that the websites listed above are suitable for children, that they have educational value, and that they contain no inappropriate material. However, because of the nature of the Internet, it is impossible to guarantee that these sites will remain active indefinitely or that their contents will not be altered.

INDEX